**GRATITUDE COMPETENCE**
*In*
**LEADERSHIP**

*© 2024 by Birgit Maria Kemphues. All rights reserved.*

No part of this publication may be reproduced, distributed, or transmitted in any form or by any means, including photocopying, recording, or other electronic or mechanical methods, without the prior written permission of the publisher, except in the case of brief quotations embodied in critical reviews and certain other non-commercial uses permitted by copyright law. For permission requests, write to the publisher, addressed "Attention: Permissions Coordinator," at the address below.

CONTACT:
Birgit Maria Kemphues
United Arab Emirates
www.instagram.com/birgit_maria_kemphues/
www.Kemphues.com

*The #1 Exquisite Exploration Bestseller*

BIRGIT MARIA KEMPHUES

# GRATITUDE COMPETENCE
## —— *In* ——
# LEADERSHIP

The Key to Unlcking Your Business's Potential

*Insightful guide tailored for current and aspiring leaders*

*For all my "we are family friends!"*

# CONTENTS

**INTRODUCTION** ........................................................... 13

*Chapter 1*
**UNDERSTANDING GRATITUDE** ..................... 16
   Defining Gratitude ....................................................... 16
   Historical Perspectives on Gratitude .................... 19
   The Science of Gratitude .......................................... 23

*Chapter 2*
**THE POWER OF GRATITUDE IN PERSONAL LIFE** ......................................................... 27
   Cultivating Gratitude Daily ....................................... 27
   Gratitude Practices and Rituals ............................. 30
   Benefits of Gratitude for Mental Health ............. 37
   Gratitude and Relationships .................................... 40

*Chapter 3*
**GRATITUDE IN BUSINESS AND LEADERSHIP** ........................................................... 48
   Why Gratitude Is Good for Business ................... 48
   The Role of Gratitude in Effective Leadership .. 52
   Strategies for Integrating Gratitude into Organizational Culture ............................................. 55

## Chapter 4
## GRATEFUL CUSTOMER RELATIONSHIPS: BUILDING LOYALTY AND LONGEVITY ..... 75

The Impact of Gratitude on Customer Experience ............................................................. 75

Techniques for Showing Appreciation to Customers ............................................................. 82

Sustaining Gratitude Practices Over Time ......... 93

Common Obstacles to Gratitude ....................... 104

Strategies for Overcoming Negativity ............... 109

Dealing with Gratitude Objectors ...................... 116

## CONCLUSION ....................................................... 123

## THE AUTHOR: ...................................................... 127

*Gratitude isn't just good manners;
it's the linchpin of prosperity.*

BIRGIT MARIA KEMPHUES

# INTRODUCTION

In the relentless pursuit of success, we're often caught in a whirlwind of ambition and hustle. It's easy to get lost in the noise, to be swept away by the endless chase for more. But there's a force, a subtle yet powerful force, that can anchor us amidst this storm: GRATITUDE. This isn't just another catchphrase; it's not ephemeral or superficial—it's the compass that points us toward our true north.

Picture yourself standing at the edge of a vast forest, the sun casting dappled shadows on the forest floor. Each tree stands tall, its roots anchored deep into the earth. But what if I told you that beneath the soil, hidden from view, lies a network of interconnected roots—a mycelial web that sustains the entire ecosystem? Gratitude is that mycelium, weaving through the fabric of our lives, connecting us to our purpose, our relationships, and our businesses.

Gratitude is the quiet revolution.

In this book, we'll embark on a journey—a pilgrimage of the heart—where we'll explore the transformative power of gratitude. We'll peel back the layers of our busy lives, revealing the raw, unfiltered essence of what truly matters. Whether you're an entrepreneur, a dreamer, or simply someone seeking more fulfillment, this book is your compass, your lantern in the dark.

Together, we'll learn how to:

- ✓ **Why Gratitude is Essential and How to Cultivate it as a Daily Habit:** Imagine gratitude as a muscle—one that grows stronger with practice. We'll flex it, stretch it, and watch it transform our days from mundane to miraculous.

- ✓ **Unleash Abundance:** Gratitude isn't just about saying "thank you." It's about opening our arms wide to receive the gifts life offers—the opportunities, the setbacks, and the unexpected blessings.

- ✓ **Navigate Storms with Grace:** Life isn't always sunshine and rainbows. But gratitude equips us with an umbrella—a shield against despair. When the storms rage, we'll dance in the rain, knowing that growth lies in the tempest.

- ✓ **Elevate Your Business:** Yes, gratitude has a boardroom seat. It's the secret sauce that fuels innovation, fosters collaboration, and turns customers into advocates. When you start your day with gratitude, you set the tone for openness and positivity in your business. You see opportunities instead of obstacles. You find lessons in failures and humility in successes. Gratitude turns what we have into enough and more. It transforms denial into acceptance, chaos into order, confusion into clarity.

We'll explore helpful case studies/stories where gratitude transformed the bottom line, and we'll provide actionable strategies for replicating these successes within your own business.

So, dear business owner, fasten your seatbelt. The journey begins. Let's unlock the vault of gratitude, dust off its golden key, and step into a world where abundance flows, connections deepen, and potential ignites. Welcome to the revolution.

*Chapter 1*

# UNDERSTANDING GRATITUDE

*"Gratitude is not only the greatest of virtues but the parent of all others."*

– Marcus Tullius Cicero.

## Defining Gratitude

Gratitude is not just about saying 'thank you.' It's an attitude, a mindset, a way of life! It's about recognizing the value in every experience, every person, and every moment. When you're grateful, you're not just happier; you're more present, more productive, and you're putting out that positive energy that attracts success.

Think about a time when someone gave you a shoutout on social media for your work. That's a moment of gratitude right there. It's not just about feeling good; it's about creating a chain reaction. You acknowledge their praise, maybe share their post, and boom – you've just spread that positivity further.

Or consider a business scenario. You've got a team member who's been crushing it, going above and beyond. You take a moment in a meeting to highlight their hard work. That's gratitude in action. It boosts morale, encourages others, and sets a culture where everyone feels valued and motivated.

In essence, gratitude is about recognizing that every person you meet, every challenge you face, is an opportunity to grow and give back. When you meet someone new, whether it's a colleague, a client, or even a stranger on the street, there's a chance to learn something new, to expand your network, or to simply enjoy a moment of human connection. That's gratitude in action – acknowledging the value that others bring into your life.

Now, when it comes to challenges, they're often seen as obstacles, but with gratitude, they become opportunities. A difficult project at work, for instance, is a chance to push your limits, to innovate, and to come out stronger on the other side. By being grateful for these moments, you're not just overcoming hurdles; you're building resilience and setting yourself up for future success.

Gratitude is also about seeing the glass not just half full, but refillable. Here's what I mean: Seeing the glass as refillable is a powerful perspective. It's about understanding that resources – be they time, energy, or creativity – are not finite. With gratitude, you recognize that there's always more to give and more to receive. It's an endless cycle of positive exchange that fuels growth and prosperity.

And these, my friend, is the key to unlocking not just your life and business's potential, but the potential of those around you. Because gratitude is contagious, and when you embody it i.e. your positive attitude and willingness to give back, it inspires those around you to do the same. It creates a ripple effect that can transform the culture of a business, uplift a community, or even change the world.

So, by defining gratitude in this manner, you're not just unlocking your own potential; you're opening doors for yourself and everyone around you. This paves the way for a legacy of positivity that transcends mere profits and KPIs, fostering a life and a business of genuine significance.

# Historical Perspectives on Gratitude

Gratitude has been a powerful force throughout history, shaping cultures and philosophies across the globe. It epitomizes the essence of positive energy, akin to the original source. Ancient civilizations had it dialed in; they knew that giving thanks was crucial for a harmonious society. Whether it was the Greeks praising the gods or Eastern traditions emphasizing harmony with nature, gratitude was the glue keeping communities tight.

Gratitude has indeed been a cornerstone in the foundation of many ancient civilizations, acting as a social adhesive that fostered community cohesion and individual well-being.

In Ancient Egypt, for instance, the concept of ma'at—harmony and balance—was central to their worldview. Gratitude was a critical aspect of maintaining this balance, elevating one's life journey and ensuring a favorable judgment in the afterlife. The Egyptians practiced rituals like the Five Gifts of Hathor, which encouraged daily gratitude, reminding individuals of the good in their lives despite any hardships.

Similarly, in Ancient Greece, gratitude was a virtue extolled by philosophers like Plato and Aristotle. It was seen as a moral duty and a necessary response to the benevolence of the gods and fellow humans. This sense of thankfulness was not just personal but woven into the very fabric of society through festivals and public ceremonies.

In Eastern traditions, such as those found in ancient China, gratitude was often linked with Confucianism, which emphasized inner virtue, morality, and respect for the community and its values. Gratitude in these societies was about maintaining harmony with nature and the cosmos, reflecting a deep understanding of the interconnectedness of all things.

These historical perspectives show that gratitude is more than just a feeling; it's a practice that has shaped human interaction and societal development. It's the recognition of the interdependence between individuals and the world around them, fostering a spirit of cooperation and mutual respect. By looking back at these ancient practices, we can see how gratitude has always been a powerful force for creating stronger communities and enriching the human experience.

Fast forward to the Renaissance, and gratitude gets intellectual. Thinkers are starting to see it as a moral guide or a tool to help navigate the complexities and challenges of human relationships and interactions.

Imagine you're a sailor in choppy waters, right? Your moral compass is Gratitude. It helps you navigate, find your way, and stay on course. It helps you maneuver the difficulties, conflicts, and uncertainties that often arise in human relationships. It's about recognizing the good in others and paying it forward. This is a cycle of goodness that keeps the ship afloat.

Speaking of paying it forward, that's the Renaissance's gift to the future. It's about creating a chain reaction of kindness. You help someone out, they help someone else, and boom – you've got a whole sea of people making waves of positive change.

Now, let's talk about modern times. Gratitude is the secret weapon for crushing it in life and business. It's about acknowledging your journey, the people who've helped you along the way, and the lessons learned from every hustle. It's not just about being thankful; it's about using that energy to fuel your passion and drive.

Take the example of the former CEO of Campbell's Soup Company, Douglas Conant. He's known for having written over 30,000 thank-you notes to his employees during his tenure. This wasn't just about being polite; it was a strategic move that helped to create a culture of appreciation within the company. By acknowledging the hard work and dedication of his team, Conant fostered a sense of belonging and motivation that translated into better performance and loyalty.

This act of gratitude turned the challenges of a global business into opportunities for personal connection and growth. Employees felt valued and seen, which is crucial in any work environment. It's a testament to how a mindset of gratitude can indeed define success, transforming the workplace into a space where people are not only recognized for their contributions but are also inspired to continue contributing to the team's success.

Gratitude isn't just a chapter in history; it's the narrative that can define success. Think of it as this intellectual force that powered some of the greatest minds of the Renaissance and the ancient civilizations. It's what helped them to see beyond themselves, to create art, science, and a society that values the good in everyone. That's the kind of vibe we need to channel today. Let's spread that sort of gratitude and make some waves of our own.

# The Science of Gratitude

In this section, let's dive into the science of gratitude and how it's not just feel-good fluff, but a powerful catalyst for transformation, both personally and professionally.

Gratitude works its Magic on the Brain first off. Again, it isn't just about being polite. It's a mindset that can literally rewire your brain. When you're grateful, your brain releases dopamine and serotonin. These are the feel-good neurotransmitters that boost your mood and make you feel all warm and fuzzy inside. It's like giving your brain a high-five for the good stuff happening around you. This not only improves your own happiness but can also uplift others. It's contagious, like a viral tweet that spreads positivity far and wide.

Gratitude undoubtedly exerts a profound influence on our brains. One such example is the practice of gratitude journaling, which has been shown to have lasting effects on the brain. In a study, participants who wrote down things they were grateful for each day exhibited increased activity in the prefrontal cortex, the area of the brain associated with decision-making and learning, when they felt more grateful months later.

Another example involves employees in a workplace setting. When managers express gratitude for their team's efforts, it not only boosts morale but also increases productivity. Employees feel valued and are more engaged, leading to a more positive work environment and better overall performance.

These instances serve not just as a testament to the science of gratitude and its tangible benefits in real-world applications, but also as compelling evidence that gratitude is more than just a social nicety; it's a powerful tool that can enhance our mental and emotional well-being, reshape our neural pathways, and improve our interactions with others.

To further highlight the importance of gratitude in today's dog-eat-dog business world, where competition is fierce and the stakes are through the roof, here are a few key facts you need to keep in mind:

- Enhanced Employee Well-being Gratitude can significantly improve employees' psychological health, reducing feelings of burnout and increasing job satisfaction. This is because gratitude activates the brain's reward system, releasing neurotransmitters like dopamine and serotonin that promote feelings of well-being, as I mentioned earlier.

- Increased Resilience Employees who regularly practice gratitude tend to develop greater resilience against stress and adversity. This is linked to gratitude's ability to enhance the brain's neural modulation of the stress hormone cortisol.

- Improved Relationships Gratitude fosters better workplace relationships. When leaders express appreciation, it can lead to stronger bonds and a more cooperative team environment. This is partly due to the release of oxytocin, a hormone that enhances social bonding and trust.

- Boosted Productivity Studies have shown that gratitude can lead to higher levels of productivity. When employees feel valued, they are more motivated and engaged, which translates into better performance and output.

- Positive Organizational Culture Gratitude contributes to a positive organizational culture, which can attract and retain talent. A culture that values appreciation is often seen as more supportive and can be a key differentiator in competitive industries.

In essence, the science of gratitude in business is about leveraging our understanding of human behavior and brain chemistry to create a more positive, productive, and fulfilling work environment.

So, when you're grinding away, remember to take a moment to reflect on what's going well. Gratitude isn't just nice to have; it's a must-have. It's the key to unlocking not just a happier life, but a more successful business. Keep it real, keep it grateful, and watch how it transforms everything around you. That's the science of gratitude, and it's very powerful.

*Chapter 2*

# THE POWER OF GRATITUDE IN PERSONAL LIFE

*Gratitude makes sense of our past, brings peace for today, and creates a vision for tomorrow."*

– Melody Beattie.

## Cultivating Gratitude Daily

Gratitude isn't just the occasional nod of appreciation; it's the steady rhythm that orchestrates the dance of our lives, guiding our steps with humility and grace. Cultivating it daily means finding those little moments, those everyday interactions, and flipping the script to see the good. It's about making gratitude as habitual as your morning coffee. And when you do that? You unlock potential you didn't even know you had. And then you start seeing opportunities instead of obstacles.

Imagine you're a barista at a busy coffee shop. It's early morning, the line is out the door, and you're feeling the heat. Now, you could focus on the stress, the endless orders, the impatient customers. Or, you could flip the script.

You start noticing the small things: the regular who always smiles, the way the morning light hits the counter, the aroma of fresh coffee. You take a moment to savor these, and gratitude starts to replace the stress. You're thankful for the job that supports you, the co-workers who have your back, and even the customers who challenge you because they push you to be better.

As this mindset takes hold, it becomes as routine as making that perfect espresso shot. And something shifts. You're no longer just a barista; you're a craftsman, an integral part of someone's morning ritual. You start seeing the coffee shop as a community hub, a place of connection. You think, "What if we started a 'pay it forward' chain?" So, you suggest it, and it takes off. Now, you're not just serving coffee; you're creating a movement of kindness.

That's the power of cultivating gratitude daily. It transforms your perspective, turning everyday interactions into opportunities for growth and connection. It's about recognizing that every moment, no matter how small, holds potential. When you embrace gratitude, you open doors to new possibilities, and life becomes richer for it.

See, the key is this: when you start living with gratitude, you're not just happier; you're more connected. You're as well building bridges with every 'thank you,' and every nod of appreciation. It's about recognizing that every person you meet, every experience you have, is an opportunity to grow, to learn, to expand your network.

So, what's the actionable step? It's simple: start by finding the good in every situation. No matter how small it seems, there's potential there. A chance to learn, to connect, to make a difference. And when you do that, when you really embrace gratitude, you're not just opening doors; you're blowing them wide open. New possibilities, new opportunities, they're all around you, waiting for you to grab them.

Life becomes richer, not in the bank account sense (although that can happen too), but in the moments, the memories, the connections. That's the richness I'm talking about. That's the absolute game-changer when you commit to cultivating gratitude every single day.

## Gratitude Practices and Rituals

When we talk about Gratitude Practices and Rituals, we're talking about the daily grind, the hustle, the things that keep you grounded while you're reaching for the stars. It's about setting up systems that ensure you're always looking at what you've got, instead of what you don't.

It's like this: You've got your eyes on the prize - reaching for the stars, but you can't forget about the launchpad. That's your gratitude. It's what keeps you grounded, keeps you focused. It's easy to get caught up in what's missing, what you're chasing. But what about what's right in front of you? What about what you've already got?

This underscores the importance of setting up systems in your life that make gratitude as routine as brushing your teeth. It's not a one-off; it's a daily ritual. It's looking at your hard-earned success, the people who support you, the opportunities you have, and simply saying, 'Wow, I'm truly grateful for all of this.'

And when you do that, when you make gratitude a ritual, something you do without even thinking, that's when you start seeing everything as an opportunity. That's when you start appreciating the process, not just the outcome. So, here's your blueprint to not just practice gratitude, but to make it a ritual:

1. **The 'Thank You' Walk:** Start your day with a walk. No phone, no distractions. Just you and your thoughts.

    Now, as you're walking, I want you to do something powerful. Every single step you take, I want you to think of one thing you're grateful for. It could be anything - from the sunrise painting the sky, to the cup of coffee waiting for you at home. Just soak it in, feel it.

    Think of this like a walking meditation, but with an added bonus - you're getting those steps in. It's a double whammy of gratitude and fitness. And let me tell you, starting your day with a mindset of gratitude sets the tone for everything else. It's like fuel for your soul, powering you through whatever the day throws your way.

So, lace up those shoes, hit the pavement, and let the 'Thank You' Walk work its magic. Trust me, you'll thank yourself later.

2. **The Five-Minute Journal:** This isn't merely a diary; it's a potent tool, poised to revolutionize your day.

So here's the drill: first thing in the morning, grab that journal, and jot down three things you're grateful for. I'm talking real stuff here, not just superficialities. Think deep, dig into those moments that make life worth living.

Then, boom, hit them with three things that would make today absolutely killer. I'm talking goals, aspirations, dreams - whatever gets your blood pumping. Set the tone for the day. Manifest that greatness.

But wait, that's not all. You got to throw in a daily affirmation, alright? Something to pump yourself up, to remind yourself that you're an absolute rockstar and you can crush anything that comes your way. Repeat after me: "I am unstoppable. I am a force to be reckoned with. I am destined for greatness."

Now, fast forward to the end of the day. Crack open that journal again, and reflect on three amazing things that happened. I don't care if it's big or small; find those moments of pure awesomeness and jot them down. It's like reliving the highlights of your day, reminding yourself that life is full of blessings.

3. **The Gratitude Trigger:** This thing right here is next-level, trust me. It's like hacking your brain for happiness, turning everyday actions into moments of gratitude.

Here's how it works: pick a simple action, something you do every single day without even thinking about it. It could be opening a door, taking a sip of water, or even tying your shoelaces. Whatever floats your boat.

Now, here's the thing: every time you do that action, I want you to pause. Stop dead in your tracks and think of one thing you're grateful for. It could be anything - the smile from a loved one, the sound of birds chirping outside your window, or even the cozy feeling of your favorite sweater wrapped around you.

That consistent act of cultivating habits is key. Training your brain to find gratitude in the everyday moments. And believe me, it's a game-changer. It's like sprinkling a little bit of joy into your day, one action at a time.

So, the next time you crack open a door or take a sip of water, remember to hit that gratitude trigger. Trust me, it'll change the way you see the world.

4. **The Gratitude Jar:** Ever wondered what a jar could do for your mood? Well, this isn't your average jar – it's your own personal stash of positivity. Every single time something good happens, I want you to write it down on a piece of paper. Big wins, small victories, moments of pure joy - it all goes in the jar. Fold it up, and drop it in. Boom, just like that, you're building your own little treasure chest of positivity.

But here's where it gets really cool. When life throws you a curveball, when you're feeling like the weight of the world is on your shoulders, I want you to reach for that jar. Pull out a note, unfold it, and soak it in. Remind yourself of the good times, my friend. Let those moments of happiness wash over you like a warm wave.

It's like having a secret weapon against negativity, right in the palm of your hand. Because no matter how tough things may seem, no matter how dark the clouds may get, you've got a jar full of sunshine waiting to lift you back up.

So, do well to grab yourself a jar, start filling it with those little nuggets of goodness, and watch how it changes your perspective on life.

5. **Think about someone in your life who's really made a difference, okay?** Maybe it's a mentor who's helped you navigate your career, a friend who's been there for you through thick and thin, or a family member who's always had your back.

Now, I want you to do something special for them. I want you to sit down and write them a letter. Not just any letter, though - a letter pouring out your heart, expressing your gratitude in every word. Tell them how much they mean to you, how they've impacted your life in ways they might not even realize.

Now, here's the twist: you're not going to stop there. Oh no, we're taking this to the next level. You're going to deliver that letter in person. Imagine yourself standing at their doorstep, letter in hand, observing their reaction as they absorb your words.

Trust me, there's something incredibly powerful about seeing their faces light up, their eyes welling up with tears, as they realize just how much they mean to you. It's a moment of pure connection, a moment that reminds you of the beauty of human relationships.

So, anytime you feel grateful for someone in your life, don't just send them a text or shoot them an email. Write them a letter, deliver it in person, and watch as the magic unfolds. I guarantee you, it'll be a moment you both cherish forever.

6. **The Gratitude Alarm:** It's time to kick your gratitude game up a notch. And here's how you do it:

Whip out your phone right now and you're set some random alarms. I am not talking about your typical wake-up call here. No, no, I'm talking about alarms with labels like 'What are you grateful for right now?' Yes, you read that right.

Now, when that alarm goes off, I want you to stop dead in your tracks. I want you to pause whatever you're doing and answer that question. What are you grateful for in this moment? It could be anything. This will help bring mindfulness into your day and train your brain to seek out the good stuff, even in the midst of chaos.

So, go ahead and set those alarms. Let them surprise you throughout the day, and watch as they transform your outlook on life. Because when you take a moment to count your blessings, everything else just falls into place.

Keep in mind that these aren't just 'nice-to-haves.' These are the tools that keep you sane, that keep you hungry, that keep you humble. They're what separates the people who have a moment from the people who make a movement. So, implement these rituals, make them as much a part of your day as breathing. Think of gratitude as a muscle – the more you work it, the stronger it gets. And before you know it, you're not just practicing it; you're living it. That's how you unlock your fullest potential.

## Benefits of Gratitude for Mental Health

Gratitude is like this superpower that doesn't get enough credit. Incorporating it into our daily lives can have profound effects on our mental health.

When you practice gratitude consistently, you're basically training your mind to focus on the positive. It's like doing reps at the gym but for your mental health.

Eventually, you start noticing the small wins, the everyday blessings, and that shifts your whole perspective. It's like, instead of getting bogged down by the one deal that fell through, you're grateful for the nine that worked out. That mindset? It reduces stress, anxiety, and all that negative noise that can cloud your judgment.

Imagine you're a content creator on social media. You've been working hard, putting out content consistently, but one day, you post a video you're really proud of and it doesn't perform as expected. You could dwell on that one "failed" post, or you could shift your perspective with gratitude.

Here's where the small wins come in. Maybe that video didn't get the views, but you notice your overall follower count has been steadily growing. People are engaging more with your content, leaving comments, and sharing your work. These are the everyday blessings that show progress and impact, beyond just the numbers on a single post.

By focusing on these positives, you maintain a healthier mindset. You're less stressed about the performance of any one post and more appreciative of the community you're building. This gratitude for the small wins keeps you motivated, reduces anxiety, and helps you make better, clearer decisions about your content strategy moving forward.

In business, this could be akin to an entrepreneur who faces a setback with a product launch. Instead of fixating on what went wrong, they choose to be grateful for the lessons learned, the customer feedback received, and the sales that did happen. This gratitude helps them refine their approach, improve their product, and come back stronger.

In both cases, gratitude acts as a tool for maintaining mental equilibrium, fostering a sense of contentment, and promoting a healthier, more positive mental state. It's a simple yet powerful way to support our mental health while pursuing our professional goals.

On the flip side, let's see what happens to that content creator and entrepreneur who fails to practice gratitude…

Content Creator without Gratitude: He/She fixates on the negative. Dwells on the underperforming posts, which leads to self-doubt and a decline in mental health. The lack of gratitude may cause them to overlook valuable feedback and miss opportunities for growth. They're more prone to burnout, anxiety, and disconnection from their audience.

Entrepreneur without Gratitude: He or She may likely view the same failed launch as a disaster. They may become overwhelmed by negative emotions, leading to increased stress and potential mental health issues. This perspective can cloud their judgment, making it harder to bounce back and negatively impacting their business and personal lives.

Examining these instances, it becomes evident that gratitude is the differentiator that enhances mental health and business potential. Undoubtedly, it allows individuals to maintain a positive outlook, improve relationships, and handle setbacks with grace and resilience. So, embracing gratitude for the small wins and everyday blessings doesn't just feel good; it's a strategic move that fosters resilience, promotes a positive work environment, and drives sustainable success. It's about seeing the glass half full, learning from every experience, and using that knowledge to propel yourself and your business forward.

## Gratitude and Relationships

Gratitude in relationships means acknowledging that every interaction is a chance to learn, to grow, to give back. It's not about the grand gestures or the flashy gifts; it's about being thankful for the person in front of you, for their time, their words, their presence in your life. And it's not just lip service; it's about showing up, being present, and giving your all.

When you're grateful, you're not keeping score. You're not in it for what you can get out of it. You're in it for the connection, the shared experiences, the journey together. That's powerful. That's what builds trust, respect, and a bond that can withstand the ups and downs.

In this section, let's explore tangible examples of gratitude within various types of relationships, drawn from real-life experiences:

- **Family Relationship:** Picture this scenario. You've got this parent, hustling hard day in and day out, grinding to provide for their family. And then there's this kid, buried in schoolwork, trying to navigate their way through the maze of education. Time, it's a precious commodity; they don't have an abundance of it. But here's the magic: they make every single moment count.

    Now, how do they do it? Well, let me break it down for you. Expressing gratitude isn't just about flashy toys or extravagant vacations, no! It's about something much deeper, much more meaningful. It's about being present, truly present. When they're together, that parent isn't checking their phone every two seconds or zoning out to some distant place. No, they're there, fully at the moment, soaking in every word, every laugh, every frown of that child.

And let me tell you, that's where the real gold is. It's in those little conversations after school, where the child spills their heart out about their day. It's in those moments of shared laughter and inside jokes. It's in those times when that parent looks at their child with eyes full of pride and appreciation, celebrating even the tiniest victories.

That's how you genuinely build a bond, my friend. Not through material things, but through something far more precious – mutual respect and love. It's about showing up, day in and day out, not just physically, but emotionally too. It's about being each other's biggest cheerleaders, supporting and lifting each other up every step of the way.

So, remember this: in a world that's constantly pulling us in a million different directions, the greatest gift you can give your family is your undivided attention. So be present, be engaged, and watch as your relationships with them flourish like never before.

- **School Relationship:** Picture this. You've got a student, grinding away at their studies, but hitting a wall with a particular subject. And then there's this teacher, not just punching the clock, but genuinely invested in seeing their students succeed.

Now, here's where the magic unfolds. That teacher doesn't just brush off the struggling student, no. They go that extra mile; they take that extra time to sit down and break things down in a way that clicks for that student. They're not just teaching, they're mentoring, they're guiding.

And how does that student respond? Well, they could easily just shrug it off, right? But no, they show gratitude in the most powerful way possible. Not with some grand gesture or fancy gift, but by rolling up their sleeves and getting down to work. They actively engage in the learning process, they soak up that teacher's advice like a sponge, and they start to see real improvement.

Now, let me tell you, as a teacher, there's nothing more fulfilling than seeing your students take what you've given them and run with it. It's like watching a seed you've planted grow into a mighty oak tree. That student's progress, it's like fuel for the teacher's fire. It motivates them to keep pushing, to keep supporting, to keep making a difference.

And what you've got here, my friend, is more than just a student-teacher relationship. It's a partnership, it's a collaboration. It's a nurturing educational environment where both parties are growing and evolving together. It's about lifting each other up, pushing each other forward, and celebrating each other's victories.

So, whether you're the student or the teacher, remember this: it's not just about the grades or the lesson plans. It's about the connections you make, the impact you have, and the growth you inspire in each other. That's the beauty of education.

- **Love Relationship:** Think of a couple who are in it for the long haul, riding the waves of life together. But hey, life, it's not always sunshine and rainbows, is it? Sometimes, it throws you a curveball, knocks you down a peg or two.

    Now, imagine one partner's had a rough day, just feeling like they're carrying the weight of the world on their shoulders. And there's the other partner, maybe they don't have all the answers, maybe they can't magically make everything better, but you know what they can do? They can be there. They can offer a shoulder to lean on, a hug to say, "Hey, I've got you," or simply an ear to listen.

See, that's the real deal right there. It's not about trying to fix everything with material stuff or distracting each other from the pain. No, it's about showing gratitude in its purest form – by being present, by acknowledging each other's struggles, and by offering unwavering support.

And as you may already know, that's what builds a rock-solid foundation for a love that can weather any storm. It's about strengthening that emotional connection, deepening that bond, and creating a partnership that can stand tall in the face of life's toughest challenges.

So, whether you're in a relationship or looking for one, remember this: it's not just about the grand gestures or the fancy dates. It's about being there for each other, through thick and thin, through the highs and the lows. That's where the true magic of love lies. That's how you build something real, something lasting.

In each of these contexts, gratitude is shown through actions and presence, creating a positive feedback loop that enhances the relationship. It's about the consistent, small acts of kindness and recognition that accumulate over time to form a deep, enduring connection.

Irrespective of the relationship type, gratitude stands as a universal virtue that enriches every relational bond. In workplace relationships, it fosters a culture of appreciation and teamwork, as colleagues and leaders recognize each other's contributions (more of this in the next chapter). In friendships, expressing gratitude strengthens bonds and deepens trust, making friends feel valued and respected. Mentor-mentee relationships thrive on gratitude, with mentors feeling fulfilled by their impact and mentees feeling supported and empowered. In community relationships, gratitude builds social cohesion and encourages acts of kindness and support. Even in casual encounters, such as with service workers or strangers, a simple expression of gratitude can uplift spirits and spread positivity. Across all these interactions, gratitude acts as a catalyst for mutual respect, generosity, and stronger connections.

So, if you want to unlock your life's potential, start with gratitude. Start with the people around you. Recognize their value, tell them they matter, and watch how it transforms your relationships. It's not rocket science; it's human science. It's understanding that gratitude is the currency of human connection, and it's priceless.

*Chapter 3*

# GRATITUDE IN BUSINESS AND LEADERSHIP

*Gratitude is a currency that we can mint for ourselves, and spend without fear of bankruptcy."*

- Fred De Witt Van Amburgh.

## Why Gratitude Is Good for Business

Gratitude in business? It's everything. It's the difference between a one-time sale and a lifetime customer. It's what turns employees into family. Why? Because gratitude is the ultimate ROI. It's not soft; it's practical. You show gratitude to your customers by listening to their feedback, by over-delivering on your promise. That's how you build a brand. it's the secret sauce of business success. It's what makes you stand out in a sea of sameness. When you're grateful, you're not just another company; you're a movement, a brand that resonates on a human level.

Why is it good for business? Because it's authentic. It's real. And in a world where everyone's trying to sell something, authenticity is rare. It's what makes people stop and listen. Gratitude shows your customers that they're not just transactions; they're part of your story. And when they feel that, they don't just buy; they become ambassadors.

Mind you, this isn't just external; it's internal too. Show gratitude to your team, and you'll see a shift. You'll see people who are motivated, who are driven not just by paychecks, but by purpose. They'll go the extra mile not because they have to, but because they want to. That's how you build a culture of excellence.

Now, picture this: a tech startup, right? They're not the first to the game; they've got competition everywhere. But here's where they flip the script. Every time a user gives feedback, they don't just listen; they act on it. They send a personal thank you note, maybe even swag, no strings attached. That's gratitude. It's not a transaction; it's a relationship.

Customers feel heard, valued, and bam! They're not just users; they're fans, they're advocates.

Now, inside the company, it's the same deal. The CEO doesn't stay in some ivory tower; they're on the ground, giving props for the late nights, the big wins, and even the tries that miss the mark. They know names, they know stories, they invest in dreams. Employees? They're not clocking in and out; they're part of something bigger. They're not just working for a paycheck; they're working for a purpose, for a mission. That's gratitude.

This goes beyond mere sentimentality; it's strategic. It's what sets this startup apart. They're not just selling a product; they're building a community. They're not just a company; they're a movement. Gratitude is their edge, their brand, their identity. It's what makes them real in a world of fakes. And that's everything.

On the other hand, here are some instances where a lack of gratitude can negatively impact a business:

- Employee Turnover: Without gratitude, employees may feel undervalued and unappreciated, leading to high turnover rates. This not only disrupts the workflow but also increases costs related to hiring and training new staff.

- Diminished Team Spirit: A workplace devoid of gratitude can result in a toxic environment where teamwork and morale are low. Employees are less likely to assist each other, which can hamper productivity and the overall success of projects.

- Stagnant Innovation: Gratitude encourages people to go above and beyond. In its absence, employees are less motivated to innovate or take initiative, leading to a lack of creativity and progress within the company.

- Poor Customer Relations: Businesses that fail to show appreciation to their customers can suffer from a lack of loyalty and negative word-of-mouth, which can be detrimental to the brand's reputation and sales.

- Weak Company Culture: Gratitude is a core component of a strong company culture. Without it, the culture may become stagnant, making the company a less desirable place to work, which can affect the recruitment and retention of top talent.

- Loss of Competitive Edge: In competitive markets, businesses that do not express gratitude may lose their edge as customers and employees gravitate towards companies that value and appreciate them.

In essence, when we talk about gratitude making or breaking a business, this is what we mean. Gratitude is the ultimate return on investment because it turns customers into family and employees into believers. It's what makes a business thrive, stand out, and lead with heart. Its absence can lead to a cascade of negative outcomes that can ultimately break a business. This section aims to steer your business away from such an outcome.

## The Role of Gratitude in Effective Leadership

Leadership is not a rank or a position; it is a choice. It's the choice to look after the person to your left and to the right of you. This is where gratitude plays a pivotal role. It's not about being in charge; it's about taking care of those in your charge. And when we express gratitude, we fulfill that responsibility.

Gratitude in leadership is about recognizing that every success we have is due to the people who show up every day to turn our vision into a reality. It's about understanding that these people have the option to work elsewhere, yet they choose to work with us. For that, we must be endlessly grateful.

Take, for example, Satya Nadella, the CEO of Microsoft, who is known for transforming the company's culture with his leadership style, which heavily emphasizes gratitude. When he took over in 2014, he shifted the focus from a "know-it-all" culture to a "learn-it-all" culture, fostering an environment of growth and appreciation.

One of the initiatives under Nadella's leadership was to encourage employees to express gratitude towards their colleagues through an internal "kudos" system. This platform allows team members to publicly acknowledge and thank each other for their contributions, big or small. Given that recognition is known to fulfill a fundamental human need for appreciation and belonging, the result of this system was a significant increase in employee engagement and cooperation, as people felt their efforts were recognized and valued.

Look, this culture of recognition and value extends beyond internal operations; it also positively impacts customer service and satisfaction. When employees are engaged and cooperative, they are more inclined to deliver high-quality work and create better experiences for customers, which is essential for the long-term success of any business.

Moreover, Nadella often expresses his gratitude in company-wide emails and meetings, not just for the successes but also for the learning opportunities from failures. This approach has created a circle of safety where employees are more willing to take risks and innovate, knowing that their leader values their contribution to the company's mission.

What I refer to as the "circle of safety" is an environment where employees feel secure and supported. This feeling of security empowers them to experiment, take calculated risks, and bring forward new ideas without fear of negative repercussions for failure.

This culture of gratitude has been credited with helping Microsoft to thrive in recent years, as it encourages employees to work not just for financial gain but for a shared purpose and for each other, aligning with the company's goals and values.

When leaders like Nadella express gratitude, they send a powerful message: You matter. Your work matters. Your dedication is making a difference. And that's the kind of leadership that inspires people to stand together, to be at their best, and to drive the organization forward. That's how gratitude unlocks the true potential of any business.

On the other hand, the absence of gratitude in leadership can have a detrimental effect on an organization. Without gratitude, leaders may inadvertently foster a culture of transactional relationships, where employees feel like mere cogs in a machine, working solely for their pay. This can lead to a lack of engagement, low morale, and high turnover rates, as employees may not feel valued or connected to the company's vision.

This is akin to withholding sunlight from plants; it stunts growth, weakens structures, and leads to decay. It's a silent killer of motivation and loyalty, and without it, the very fabric of an organization can unravel.

So, if you're leading without gratitude, you're just bossing people around. And nobody wants to work for a boss. They want to work for a leader. Someone who's grateful for their team, for the opportunity to serve customers, and for the chance to make a dent in the universe. Therefore, Instead of commanding, collaborate. Instead of taking credit, give it away. That's how you build a team that's willing to go to war for you.

# Strategies for Integrating Gratitude into Organizational Culture

Integrating gratitude into organizational culture means embedding it into the very DNA of the company's operations, making it a core part of the company's values, communication, and daily practices. It's a strategic approach that can lead to increased employee engagement, higher job satisfaction, and ultimately, a more successful and resilient organization.

When you build a culture that breathes gratitude, you're not just making people feel good—you're driving results. This culture of gratitude is built on the understanding that every team member, regardless of their role, is valuable and that their work has a meaningful impact on the success of the business.

This section of the book offers a comprehensive, step-by-step guide to seamlessly integrating gratitude into the culture of your organization. Here's a breakdown of the steps:

1. **Lead by Example:** If you're running the show, whether you're the CEO, the manager, or the team leader, you've got a responsibility that goes beyond just hitting targets and making decisions. You have to set the tone. And just so you know, gratitude needs to be a big part of that tone.

    See, it's not enough to just bark orders and expect everyone to fall in line. If you want your team to give their all, day in and day out, you've got to show them that you appreciate their hustle. And I'm not talking about some half-hearted "thanks" thrown their way every now and then. No, I'm talking about genuine, heartfelt appreciation for the blood, sweat, and tears they're putting into the game.

So, how do you do it? Well, first off, you've got to make gratitude a part of your leadership style. That means you have to walk the walk, not just talk the talk. Show your team that you're grateful for their efforts by expressing it loud and clear, both publicly and frequently.

When someone on your team goes above and beyond, don't just let it slide. Call them out, and give them a shoutout in front of the whole crew. Let them know that you see their hard work and you appreciate it. And hey, don't be stingy with the praise. Spread it around like confetti at a celebration.

But here's the thing, it's not just about the big wins. It's about recognizing the little victories too. So, if someone hits a deadline ahead of schedule, let them know you noticed. It's these small moments of appreciation that add up and make a real difference in how your team feels about their work.

And I get it. Sometimes things get hectic, and it's easy to forget to show gratitude amidst the chaos. But trust me, taking a minute out of your day to acknowledge someone's hard work is never a waste of time. In fact, it's one of the best investments you can make in your team's morale and motivation.

So, lead by example, my friend. Show your team what gratitude looks like in action. Because when you do, you'll not only inspire them to keep hustling but you'll also create a culture where appreciation is the name of the game. And let me make it clear to you, that's a culture where magic happens.

2. **Create Rituals:** Rituals are powerful tools for embedding gratitude into daily work life. When I mention ritual, I'm talking about creating traditions, routines, and habits that make gratitude a non-negotiable part of your team's daily life.

    Picture this: you walk into the office every morning, and the first thing you do isn't checking emails or grabbing coffee, it's expressing gratitude. That's right, we're talking about starting your day with a gratitude round.

Imagine gathering your team for a quick huddle and kicking things off by each person sharing one thing they're grateful for. It could be something work-related, like a successful project, or something personal, like spending time with family over the weekend. Whatever it is, taking a moment to pause and reflect on what you're thankful for sets a positive tone for the day ahead.

But rituals aren't just about what happens in the morning. They're about weaving gratitude into the fabric of your team's interactions throughout the day. That's where the shout-out board comes in.

Imagine having a dedicated space in your office where team members can publicly acknowledge each other's contributions. Whether it's a sticky note on a bulletin board or a digital platform where kudos are shared, the idea is the same: to celebrate wins, big and small, and show appreciation for your colleagues' hard work.

And let's not forget about the power of handwritten thank-you notes. In this digital age, there's something extra special about receiving a handwritten message of gratitude. So why not make it a ritual? Set aside time each week to write personalized notes to team members, thanking them for their efforts and letting them know how much you appreciate their contributions.

The key here is consistency. Whether it's starting meetings with a gratitude round, keeping a shout-out board updated, or sending out thank-you notes, make these rituals a regular part of your team's routine. And don't be afraid to get creative! You could utilize the gratitude jar I talked about in the previous chapter. Creatively set up a "Gratitude Jar" in a common area of the office where team members can drop in notes of thanks and appreciation for their colleagues. Encourage everyone to take a moment each day to jot down something they're grateful for or someone they want to recognize. Then, at the end of the week or month, gather together as a team to read and celebrate the contents of the jar. It's a simple yet powerful way to foster a culture of gratitude and camaraderie.

The more personalized and meaningful your rituals are, the more impact they'll have on your team's morale and motivation. So go ahead, establish rituals that reinforce a culture of appreciation.

3. **Acknowledge Small Wins:** "Small wins, yeah. I've read that a thousand times in this book" Yes, this repetition isn't without purpose. These small wins easily go unnoticed and are often overlooked, hence the need for me to keep emphasizing them. This time, let's really talk about the power of acknowledging them.

Pay attention, because this is crucial: big wins might grab the spotlight, but it's the small wins that keep the momentum going. So, as a leader, it's your job to make sure those small wins don't fly under the radar.

Picture this: you've got a project team grinding away day in and day out, putting in the hard work to move the needle forward. Now, sure, hitting the big milestones is cause for celebration, but what about all those little victories along the way?

Maybe it's nailing a tricky presentation or finally figuring out that stubborn bug in the code. Whatever it is, those small wins matter, and they deserve to be recognized.

So, how do you do it? Well, first off, you've got to make a conscious effort to pay attention. Keep your finger on the pulse of what's happening on the ground, and be on the lookout for those moments of progress, however small they may seem.

And when you spot one? Don't just let it pass by unnoticed. Take a moment to acknowledge it, to celebrate it, to shine a spotlight on it. It could be as simple as a quick shoutout in a team meeting, a high-five in the hallway, or a congratulatory email sent to the whole team.

The key here is to make sure your team knows that you see their efforts, that you appreciate their hard work, and that you value their contributions, no matter how small. Because when you do, you're not just boosting morale and motivation; you're also reinforcing a culture of excellence and continuous improvement.

So, next time you see a team member scoring a small win, don't let it slip by unnoticed. Take a moment to celebrate it, to savor it, and to show your gratitude for all the hard work that went into making it happen. Trust me, it's these small wins that add up over time and pave the way for even bigger victories down the road.

4. **Empower Employees to Recognize Each Other:** Gratitude shouldn't be a one-way street. It's not just about leaders recognizing their team members; it's about fostering a culture where

everyone feels empowered to acknowledge and appreciate each other's efforts.

Think about it: your team members are the ones working side by side, day in and day out. They see firsthand the hard work, dedication, and creativity that their colleagues bring to the table. So why not leverage that insight and let them be the ones to shine a spotlight on each other's achievements?

That's where peer-to-peer recognition programs come into play. These programs give employees the opportunity to acknowledge and celebrate their colleagues' contributions in a meaningful way. Whether it's a simple shoutout in a team meeting, a heartfelt thank-you email, or a nomination for an employee recognition award, the idea is the same: to create a culture where appreciation is woven into the fabric of everyday interactions.

But it's not just about saying "thanks" and calling it a day. Peer-to-peer recognition programs also have the power to reinforce positive behaviors and values within your organization. When employees see their colleagues being recognized for things like collaboration, innovation, and going above and beyond, it sends a clear message about what's important and valued within the company.

And let me tell you, the ripple effects of peer-to-peer recognition can be profound. Not only does it foster a sense of camaraderie and teamwork, but it also boosts morale, engagement, and job satisfaction. When employees feel seen, heard, and appreciated by their peers, they're more likely to feel motivated, connected, and committed to their work.

So, as a leader, it's your job to encourage and support peer-to-peer recognition initiatives within your organization. Provide the tools, resources, and guidance needed to get these programs up and running, and then step back and let your team take it from there.

5. **Invest in Professional Development:** One of the most powerful ways to show gratitude to your team is by investing in their growth and development. Imagine you've got a team of rockstars – talented, motivated individuals who are ready to take on the world. They're already giving their all, but you know there's untapped potential waiting to be unleashed. So, what do you do? You invest in their development.

That means providing opportunities for training, mentorship, and skill-building that go beyond the basics. Sure, everyone needs to know how to do their job, but why stop there? Why not give them the tools they need to not just survive, but thrive?

And, how do you do this? Well, first off, you need to know your team – their strengths, their interests, their goals. Find out what makes them tick and what they're passionate about. Then, tailor your professional development initiatives to meet their individual needs and aspirations.

Maybe it's sending them to industry conferences or workshops to learn the latest trends and best practices. Maybe it's pairing them up with a mentor who can offer guidance, support, and wisdom gained from years of experience. Maybe it's providing access to online courses, certifications, or other learning resources that allow them to deepen their skills and expertise.

But it's not just about the technical stuff. It's also about investing in their personal and leadership development. That means offering workshops or coaching sessions on communication, teamwork, problem-solving, and other soft skills that are essential for success in today's workplace.

And don't forget about recognition and rewards. When someone on your team goes above and beyond, whether it's mastering a new skill, taking on a leadership role, or achieving a major milestone, make sure they know their efforts haven't gone unnoticed. Offer praise, bonuses, promotions, or other incentives to show your appreciation and encourage continued growth and excellence.

6. **Promote Work-Life Balance:** Did you know that expressing gratitude extends beyond mere appreciation to encompass valuing your employees' time, energy, and overall well-being? It's an essential insight. Yet, understanding the most effective approach to achieve this is equally important. Hence a need to promote work-life balance.

Picture this: you've got a team of dedicated professionals who are passionate about their work, but they also have lives outside of the office. They've got families, hobbies, and personal commitments that are just as important as their jobs. So, as a leader, it's your job to create an environment where they can thrive both professionally and personally.

That means offering flexible work arrangements that accommodate different lifestyles and schedules. Whether it's remote work options, flexible hours, or compressed workweeks, give your employees the freedom to manage their time in a way that works best for them. Trust me, when employees have control over their schedules, they're more likely to feel empowered, engaged, and motivated to do their best work.

But it's not just about flexibility – it's also about encouraging employees to take time off and recharge their batteries. That means promoting a culture where vacation days are seen as a valuable resource, not a sign of weakness. Encourage employees to use their vacation time to rest, relax, and rejuvenate, knowing that they'll come back refreshed and ready to tackle new challenges.

And hey, let's talk about overtime for a minute. Sure, there are times when extra hours are necessary to meet deadlines or handle emergencies. But as a leader, it's your job to make sure that overtime doesn't become the norm. Discourage a culture of overwork by setting realistic expectations, delegating tasks effectively, and encouraging employees to prioritize self-care and well-being.

Because here's the thing: when employees feel respected and valued as individuals – when they know that their organization cares about their happiness and fulfillment both inside and outside of work – they're more likely to be engaged, productive, and committed to their jobs. And let me tell you, that's a recipe for success that benefits everyone involved.

So go ahead, promote work-life balance within your organization, and watch as gratitude flourishes, morale soars, and productivity reaches new heights.

7. **Foster a Culture of Feedback:** Feedback is a gift. It's not always easy to give or receive, but when done right, it can be incredibly valuable for personal and professional growth. And here's the thing – receiving feedback graciously is an act of gratitude in itself.

Imagine you've got a team that's firing on all cylinders, but there's always room for improvement, right? That's where feedback comes in. It's about creating a culture where open and honest communication is not just encouraged, but celebrated.

So, how do you go about it? First off, you have to create channels for feedback to flow freely. Whether it's regular one-on-one meetings, anonymous surveys, suggestion boxes, or dedicated Slack channels, make sure there are multiple avenues for employees to share their thoughts, ideas, and concerns.

Though, it's not just about collecting feedback – it's also about how you respond to it. When someone takes the time to offer feedback, whether it's positive or constructive, it's important to acknowledge and appreciate their input. That means saying "thank you" – genuinely and sincerely – for taking the time to share their thoughts.

Now, let's talk about constructive criticism for a minute. It's not always easy to hear, but it's essential for growth and improvement. So, as a leader, it's your job to create a safe and supportive environment where feedback is given and received with empathy and respect.

Encourage your team to give feedback in a constructive and solution-oriented manner. Focus on specific behaviors or actions, rather than personal attacks or generalizations. And when receiving feedback, listen actively, ask clarifying questions, and express gratitude for the opportunity to learn and grow.

Also note this: feedback is a two-way street. When employees feel heard, valued, and respected, they're more likely to be engaged, motivated, and committed to their work. That's a recipe for success that benefits everyone involved.

So what are you waiting for? Start fostering a culture of feedback within your organization, and watch as gratitude flourishes, communication improves, and performance reaches new heights.

8. **Give Back to the Community:** Gratitude extends beyond the boundaries of your organization. It's about recognizing the support and opportunities provided by the community around you and showing appreciation through action.

Picture a team of talented individuals who are grateful for the opportunities they've been given. They're eager to give back and make a positive impact beyond their day-to-day work. That's where community involvement comes in. But first, you have to lead by example. Make giving back to the community a core part of your company's values and mission. Show your team that you're committed to making a difference and encourage them to do the same.

One way to do this is by supporting volunteering and community service initiatives. Whether it's organizing group volunteer events, offering paid time off for volunteering, or matching employee donations to charitable causes, find ways to make giving back a regular part of your company culture.

But it's not just about writing checks or ticking boxes – it's also about getting involved in meaningful ways. Encourage your team to roll up their sleeves and get their hands dirty, whether it's cleaning up a local park, serving meals at a homeless shelter, or mentoring underprivileged youth.

Also, let's talk about supporting causes that align with your company's values. Whether it's environmental sustainability, social justice, or education, find causes that resonate with your team and your customers, and make a real difference in your community.

Because here's the thing: giving back isn't just about altruism – it's also about gratitude. When employees see the impact they can have on the lives of others, it fosters a sense of gratitude and fulfillment that extends far beyond the walls of your organization.

Not only does giving back strengthen your company's reputation and social impact, but it also creates a sense of purpose and connection among your team members. So go ahead, give back to the community, and watch as gratitude flourishes, teamwork strengthens, and your company's impact grows exponentially.

9. **Gratitude Workshops or Training:** One final way to harness the power of gratitude is through dedicated workshops or trainings.

    You probably have a team that's hungry for growth and eager to cultivate a culture of gratitude in place. They're ready to roll up their sleeves and dive deep into what it means to truly appreciate and value one another. That's where gratitude workshops come in.

    So, how do you do this? In addition to implementing the strategies outlined in this section, you can bring in experts in this field. Invest in guest speakers, facilitators, or experts in positive psychology who can share insights, strategies, and practical tips for fostering gratitude in the workplace.

These experts can provide a wealth of knowledge and experience, drawing from the latest research and best practices in the field of positive psychology. They can offer a framework for understanding the science behind gratitude and its impact on employee well-being, engagement, and performance.

But it's not just about theory – it's also about practice. Gratitude workshops provide a safe and supportive space for your team to engage in experiential exercises and activities that bring the concept of gratitude to life.

By providing your team with the opportunity to engage in dedicated workshops or training focused on gratitude, you're not just deepening their understanding – you're empowering them to make a real difference in the workplace.

There you have it. Nine proven strategies to weave gratitude into the fabric of your organizational culture. Now is the moment to act and lay the foundation for the culture your organization truly deserves. And keep in mind, this isn't a one-time initiative; it's an ongoing commitment that requires consistency, authenticity, and intentionality. But the rewards – increased employee satisfaction, higher retention rates, and a more positive work environment – are well worth the effort. So, go ahead, start cultivating a culture of gratitude, and watch your organization thrive!

*Chapter 4*

# GRATEFUL CUSTOMER RELATIONSHIPS: BUILDING LOYALTY AND LONGEVITY

*"Gratitude is the memory of the heart."*

- Jean Baptiste Massieu

## The Impact of Gratitude on Customer Experience

Practicing gratitude transcends the transactional nature of business. When you're grateful, you're not just another company; you become a part of your customers' lives, and this helps create a bond that goes beyond the product or service offered. customers start seeing your company not just as a provider but as a partner in their journey. It's like having a friend who's always there, not just a store on the street.

Think about it. When was the last time a business made you feel like you mattered? When last did you get that VIP treatment? That's the power of gratitude. When a business makes a customer feel valued, it's not just about the immediate satisfaction; it's about creating a lasting impression. Gratitude can elevate a customer's experience from ordinary to extraordinary, making them feel very important (of course they are). This emotional connection turns a one-time buyer into a lifelong fan. It's about creating an experience so memorable that they can't help but talk about it.

Let's delve deeper into why this holds such remarkable potency:

- **Emotional Resonance:** This refers to the deep, lasting impact that experiences can have on individuals. In the context of customer interactions, it's about creating moments that evoke positive emotions and forge connections with the brand. When customers feel genuinely appreciated, whether through personalized gestures, exceptional service, or expressions of gratitude, it triggers a cascade of positive feelings.

Imagine a scenario where a customer receives a handwritten thank-you note along with their purchase, acknowledging their support and expressing genuine appreciation for their business. This simple act goes beyond the transactional nature of the interaction; it communicates that the customer is valued as an individual, not just as a source of revenue. As a result, the customer is more likely to feel a sense of warmth, satisfaction, and loyalty towards the brand.

These positive emotions become intertwined with the customer's perception of the brand, forming a strong, positive association. They remember how the brand made them feel, which can influence their future purchasing decisions and their willingness to recommend the brand to others. This emotional resonance creates a bond that transcends the functional aspects of the product or service, fostering a deeper connection between the customer and the brand.

- **Word-of-Mouth:** Happy customers are your best advocates. This is one of the most powerful and influential forms of promotion for any business. It relies on these happy and satisfied customers voluntarily sharing their positive experiences with others, such as friends, family, colleagues, or even strangers. When customers have a great experience with a brand, they often feel compelled to share it with others, acting as enthusiastic advocates or ambassadors.

Here's how this works:

- **Trust and Authenticity:** Recommendations from friends or family are often perceived as more trustworthy and authentic than traditional advertising. When someone hears about a positive experience directly from someone they trust, they're more likely to consider trying the brand themselves.

- **Expanded Reach:** Word-of-mouth has the potential to reach a wide audience. A single satisfied customer can share their experience with multiple people, who may in turn share it with others, creating a ripple effect that extends the reach of the brand far beyond its initial customer base.

- **Cost-Effectiveness:** Unlike paid advertising or marketing campaigns, word-of-mouth promotion is essentially free for the business. It relies on the quality of the customer experience rather than the size of the marketing budget. Therefore, it can be a highly cost-effective way to acquire new customers and drive growth.

- **Personalization:** Recommendations from friends or family members often come with a personal touch. When someone shares their positive experience with others, they may tailor their message to resonate with the interests or needs of the recipient, making it more compelling and persuasive.

- **Long-Term Impact:** Word-of-mouth recommendations can have a lasting impact on brand perception and reputation. Positive experiences shared by satisfied customers contribute to building a positive brand image over time, which can lead to increased customer loyalty and trust.

By prioritizing customer satisfaction and creating memorable experiences, businesses can encourage word-of-mouth promotion and turn their happy customers into loyal advocates. These advocates play a crucial role in attracting new customers, building brand awareness, and fostering long-term success. Therefore, investing in strategies to delight customers and encourage positive word-of-mouth can yield significant benefits for your business regardless of size.

- ❖ **Differentiation:** In today's crowded marketplace, where customers are bombarded with numerous options for products and services, standing out from the competition is essential for businesses to thrive.

  By the term "Differentiation", I mean distinguishing your brand from others in the minds of consumers, highlighting what makes it unique and compelling.

  Differentiation is not just about being different for the sake of it; it's about being authentically and meaningfully unique in ways that resonate with consumers. Gratitude, as a core component of this differentiation strategy, serves as a beacon, guiding businesses toward building deeper, more meaningful connections with their audience and ultimately gaining a sustainable competitive edge in the market.

- ❖ **Customer Retention:** Customer retention goes beyond the initial transaction; it's about nurturing relationships and fostering loyalty to ensure customers keep coming back. In today's competitive landscape, where customer acquisition costs can be high, retaining existing customers is more cost-effective and crucial for sustainable growth.

Gratitude plays a pivotal role in this process. When customers feel appreciated and valued, they are more likely to develop a sense of loyalty towards a brand. Genuine expressions of gratitude create positive emotional connections, reinforcing the customer's decision to choose your brand over others. Whether it's a simple thank you note, a personalized gesture, or a special offer, acknowledging and appreciating customers for their patronage fosters a sense of belonging and importance.

- ❖ **Brand Legacy:** Over time, these individual experiences contribute to your brand's legacy. People remember how you made them feel, and that's what keeps them coming back.

Furthermore, brand legacy extends beyond individual customers to encompass the broader community. How a brand engages with and contributes to society, its commitment to social responsibility, and its impact on the world—all of these factors shape its legacy in the eyes of the public.

Remember, in a world where everyone is selling something, gratitude is the currency that can buy you real estate in people's hearts. So, from today, listen, engage, and go above and beyond. Send personalized messages, remember their names, and always, always add value. Because when you give without expectation, you receive without limitation.

## Techniques for Showing Appreciation to Customers

Your customers have choices. Tons of them. They could go anywhere, but they chose you. They chose your product, your service, and your brand. And that deserves some serious recognition.

Take for example Starbucks, a global coffeehouse chain, which implemented a loyalty program that allows customers to earn stars for every purchase they make using the Starbucks app or registered Starbucks card. These stars can then be redeemed for free drinks, food, or merchandise.

What makes this program stand out is how it goes beyond just offering discounts. Starbucks utilizes personalized offers based on customers' purchase history and preferences, making them feel valued and appreciated. Additionally, they often surprise and delight customers with bonus star offers, birthday rewards, and exclusive member events.

By implementing such a program as a form of appreciation, Starbucks not only encourages repeat business but also fosters a sense of loyalty and connection with its customers. It shows that Starbucks recognizes and appreciates the choice customers make to patronize their stores over other coffee options. This highlights the power of showing appreciation in building long-term customer relationships and driving business growth. So how do you show appreciation to your own customers? Let me break it down for you.

1. Be Authentic: When you're expressing that appreciation, it has to be authentic. I'm talking from the heart, deep down. None of that fake stuff, your customers are not dumb. They can sniff out insincerity from a mile away. So, if you're going to thank someone, mean it. Show them you genuinely appreciate their support, their business, and their loyalty.

    Think of it as conversing with a friend. You wouldn't just throw out empty compliments, right? No, you'd mean every word. Same goes for your customers. They're not just numbers on a spreadsheet; they're real people who chose to spend their hard-earned money with you, which is why your 'thank you' should be coming straight from the heart.

So, don't fake it. Don't just go through the motions. Show some genuine appreciation, and watch how your customers respond.

2. Personalize Your Thanks: Every customer is unique, right? So why not make your thanks personal? I'm talking about going beyond the generic 'thank you' and really showing that you care about each and every one of them.

Think about it, since every customer is unique, they've got their own story, their own journey with your brand. So, why would you treat them all the same? No, that's not how you should do things. You have to tailor your thanks to each individual and make it resonate with them personally.

If you are dropping them a note, make sure it speaks to their specific experience with your brand. Maybe they've been a loyal customer for years, or maybe they just made their first purchase. Either way, acknowledge and appreciate it.

It's about demonstrating genuine attentiveness, not merely going through the motions. When a customer feels like you really see them, really appreciate them, that's when you build a bond that goes beyond just a transaction. That's when you create a fan, a loyal supporter who will stick with you through thick and thin.

So, do not overlook this. Take the time to personalize your thanks, and watch how it strengthens your relationships with your customers. It's a small gesture, but it can make a world of difference.

3. Engage on Social Media: Social media has become a pivotal platform for businesses to connect with their audience. It's not just a place to broadcast messages; it's where meaningful interactions and relationships are formed.

When used appropriately, it serves as an opportunity to foster a sense of community around your brand. By actively engaging with your audience, responding to comments, and participating in conversations, you can create a space where customers feel valued and connected to your brand. This demonstrates that you care about their opinions and are willing to address their concerns.

And hey, do not be afraid to give them shoutouts too. Recognize their support, their loyalty, and their love for your brand. Think of social media as a platform to make them feel special, make them feel appreciated. Because when you do that, you're not just building a customer base, you're building a community.

So, get out there, engage with your audience, and watch how it transforms your business. Social media isn't just a tool; it's a way to connect with people on a deeper level. Embrace it.

4. Reward Loyalty: Loyalty isn't just a one-way street, okay? If your customers are sticking with you through thick and thin, it's time to roll out the red carpet and give them the VIP treatment they deserve.

These sets of customers are like family. They've got your back, they support your hustle, and they keep coming back for more. So, it's only right that you show them some love in return.

How do you do that? You set up a killer loyalty program, that's how! Give them perks, give them benefits, make them feel special. Maybe it's a discount on their next purchase, maybe it's early access to new products, maybe it's exclusive access to events or content. Whatever it is, make it worth their while.

Because here's the thing: When you make your loyal customers feel like part of the family, they're going to stick around for the long haul. They're going to become your biggest advocates, your raving fans, your ride-or-dies.

So, don't sleep on this. Reward that loyalty, show your customers how much you appreciate them, and watch how it pays off in the long run. Loyalty is a two-way street, and it's time to start driving.

5. Ask for Feedback: "Want to show you value your customers? Ask them what they think. Feedback is like gold. It's pure, it's valuable. Your customers have got insights, they've got opinions, and they're not afraid to share them. So, why not tap into that? Why not harness that power?

Although, it's not just about asking for feedback; it's about doing something with it. I'm talking about taking that feedback, analyzing it, and making real changes based on it. That's when your customers see that you're not just listening, you're actually committed to being better.

Consider the popular online retailer, Amazon. Amazon has always placed a strong emphasis on customer feedback and continuously strives to improve its services based on customer input.

For instance, Amazon's product review system allows customers to leave feedback and ratings for products they have purchased. This feedback is not only valuable for other potential buyers but also for Amazon itself. The company closely monitors these feedbacks and analyzes them to identify trends, common complaints, or areas where products may need improvement.

In one instance, Amazon noticed a recurring theme in customer reviews for a particular electronics product - many customers were expressing frustration with the product's packaging, citing issues with damage during shipping. Instead of ignoring this feedback or simply acknowledging it without taking action, Amazon took proactive steps to address the problem.

Based on the feedback, Amazon worked with the manufacturer to redesign the product's packaging to provide better protection during shipping. They also updated their shipping procedures to ensure that fragile items like this one were handled with extra care.

After implementing these changes, Amazon saw a significant decrease in complaints related to damaged products in customer reviews. Customers who had previously experienced issues were pleasantly surprised by the improved packaging and began leaving positive reviews praising Amazon's responsiveness to their feedback.

Another thing to note here is this: Amazon didn't stop at implementing these changes; they also communicated back to customers. By informing customers about the improvements made in response to their feedback, Amazon closes the loop and reinforces the value of customer input. This is the cycle every business should follow in today's landscape - Asking for feedback, analyzing it, making changes, and then communicating those changes back to customers. This way, any business can demonstrate its dedication to being better and valuing its customers' opinions.

And when you show your customers that you're committed to being better, that's when you build trust, that's when you build loyalty, and that's when you build a brand that people cannot help but talk about.

6. Go the Extra Mile: Sometimes, it's the little things that count. Imagine you're a customer walking into your favorite local coffee shop. You order your usual latte, and as you're about to pay, the barista surprises you by saying, "This one's on us today, just to say thanks for being a regular!"

That's going the extra mile, my friend. It's those unexpected acts of kindness and thoughtfulness that really make a difference in customer experiences. And customers appreciate when you go above and beyond to make them feel special. It could be something as simple as throwing in a freebie or offering a discount on their next purchase. These little gestures may seem small, but they have a big impact.

When you surprise your customers with something unexpected, you're showing them that you value their business, that you're paying attention, and that you genuinely care about their satisfaction.

Let me give you an example: Think about the last time you ordered something online and received a handwritten note or a small gift along with your purchase. Didn't that make you feel appreciated? Didn't it make you want to support that business again in the future?

That's the power of going the extra mile. It's about creating memorable moments that leave a lasting impression on your customers. It's about blowing their minds with your thoughtfulness and turning them into raving fans of your brand.

So, don't underestimate the impact of those little things. Surprise your customers, delight them, and watch how it strengthens your relationships and builds loyalty in the long run.

7. **Public Recognition:** Shine a spotlight on your customers. By doing so, you're not just showing appreciation; you're creating a sense of community and belonging. It's like saying, "Hey, you're part of our family, and we want everyone to know it."

So, how do you do it? It's simple. Feature their stories, their reviews, their photos or videos on your platforms. Let them be the stars of the show for a moment. Not only does this make them feel special and appreciated, but it also shows potential customers how real people are using and loving your products or services.

Let me give you an example: Think about how Airbnb showcases guest stories and photos on its website and social media channels. They highlight the unique experiences and adventures that guests have had while staying in Airbnb accommodations. This not only adds authenticity to their brand but also encourages others to book with Airbnb to have their own memorable experiences.

And here's the best part: When you feature your customers, you're not just giving them some love; you're also getting authentic content that you can use to showcase your brand. It's a win-win situation.

So, do not shy away from putting your customers in the spotlight. Celebrate their stories, their experiences, and watch how it strengthens your relationship with them and attracts new customers to your brand.

These are just a few examples, but the key takeaway is this: customer appreciation is about making it personal, making it genuine, and always looking for ways to add value to the customer experience. That's how you turn customers into loyal fans. That's the power of gratitude in action. And remember, when you give it out, it comes back in tenfold. Keep it real always. Value the people who support your business and they'll keep coming back.

## Sustaining Gratitude Practices Over Time

Consistency is King. While you've mastered the techniques outlined in previous sections, the true magic lies in your unwavering dedication. I'm talking about turning gratitude into base instinct, making it a natural and automatic response to situations.

Gratitude, through consistent practice, can become a deeply ingrained habit, almost like a reflexive response, where you automatically feel thankful for the blessings, big or small, that you encounter.

Take, for example the "fight or flight" response. When faced with a perceived threat or danger, our body undergoes a series of automatic physiological changes aimed at preparing us to either confront the threat (fight) or flee from it (flight). This response is deeply ingrained in human biology and is governed by the autonomic nervous system, specifically the sympathetic nervous system.

When the brain perceives a threat, it sends signals to various parts of the body to release stress hormones like adrenaline and cortisol. These hormones trigger a cascade of physiological changes, including increased heart rate, heightened alertness, dilation of the pupils, and redirection of blood flow to vital organs like the muscles and brain. These changes occur automatically and rapidly, often without conscious thought, allowing individuals to react swiftly to potentially dangerous situations.

The fight or flight response is a prime example of a base instinct because it is deeply rooted in human evolution and serves as a fundamental survival mechanism. It enables us to respond quickly and effectively to threats, increasing our chances of survival in dangerous situations.

Similarly, there exists the potential to embed gratitude within our biological makeup. This essentially involves rewiring the brain through repeated positive reinforcement. Over time, the brain begins to associate various experiences with feelings of gratitude, leading to a subconscious tendency to view situations through a lens of appreciation. Here's how you do it:

1. Document the Journey: Keep a gratitude journal, not just for the good days but also for the tough ones. Reflect on your growth. It's about the journey, not just the destination.

Here's an example of how you document your journey in a gratitude journal:

Date: March 15, 2024

Gratitude Entry:

"Today was one of those days where nothing seemed to go right. I lost a major client, my car broke down, and I missed an important family event. But as I sit here with my journal, I'm reminded of the power of perspective.

Six months ago, losing a client would've broken me. But today, I'm grateful for the resilience I've built. I'm thankful for the clients who are still with me, and for the lessons this loss will teach me. I'm grateful for the mechanic who stayed late to fix my car, and for the family who understands when work gets in the way.

This isn't just a bad day; it's a testament to how far I've come. The challenges I've overcome have taught me patience, humility, and the value of hard work. They've shown me that growth often comes disguised as failure, and that gratitude can turn a setback into a step forward.

I'm documenting this not to dwell on the negative, but to celebrate the journey. To remember that every challenge is an opportunity to practice gratitude and to grow."

Documenting both the highs and lows helps you see the full picture of your personal growth and maintain a mindset of gratitude. It's not just about acknowledging the good times but also finding value and lessons in the hardships. This practice can help sustain gratitude over the long run by embedding it into the very fabric of your daily life. So, keep documenting that journey of gratitude. Live it, breathe it, embrace it.

2. Accountability Partners: Surround yourself with a community or a squad that holds you accountable. When you're slipping, they'll remind you of your 'why.' Imagine you're a marathon runner. The road is long, the weather unpredictable, and there are moments when your legs feel like giving up. This is where your running mates, your accountability partners, come into play. They're the ones running alongside you, matching your pace, reminding you of the finish line when all you can see is the endless road ahead.

Let's say you're Jane, an entrepreneur with a vision to revolutionize the way we recycle.

You've got the plan, the passion, and the drive. But some days, the weight of the work ahead makes you question if it's all worth it. That's when Tom, your long-time friend and fellow eco-warrior, steps in. He's not just there to pat you on the back; he's there to keep you grounded and focused. When you're about to skip a crucial networking event because you're swamped with paperwork, Tom is the one who sends you a text saying, "Remember why you started this. People need to hear about your idea."

Tom is your accountability partner. He's not there to do the work for you, but to ensure you don't lose sight of your 'why'. He's the one who celebrates your wins, no matter how small, and who sits with you when you're mapping out the next steps after a setback. With Tom, and others like him, you're not just working towards your goal; you're part of a community that shares your values and vision.

Accountability partners are the human reminders of your commitment to gratitude. They're the voices that help you navigate through the noise of daily life and keep you true to your path of acknowledging and appreciating the progress you make, the people you meet, and the impact you have. They're essential in sustaining gratitude because they embody the very essence of it—connection, support, and shared growth.

3. Set Gratitude Goals: Just like business targets, set gratitude milestones. Celebrate them. It's not just about the numbers; it's about the people, the experiences, the lessons learned.

This is akin to planting a garden of positivity that you cultivate and watch flourish over time. It's about creating markers along your path that remind you to pause, reflect, and celebrate the often-overlooked milestones of your emotional and spiritual growth.

For instance, imagine you're a teacher who's set a gratitude goal to recognize and appreciate the unique contributions of each student. Your milestone could be as simple as acknowledging one student each week for something that's not academically related—like their kindness, their effort to help others, or even their willingness to try despite struggling.

At the end of the term, you don't just have a list of academic achievements; you have an array of moments that celebrate the human spirit. You've created a classroom culture where gratitude is the norm, not the exception. This practice not only enriches your students' lives but also reinforces your own commitment to seeing and appreciating the value in every interaction, every challenge, and every success.

Gratitude goals are not about grand gestures; they're about the cumulative effect of many small acts of recognition and appreciation. They're about setting an intention to find joy in the journey and to make gratitude a living, breathing part of your daily life. By celebrating these milestones, you're not just counting your blessings; you're multiplying them.

4. Reflect and Reset: Reflecting and resetting is like being the captain of a ship on the vast ocean of life. The sea is ever-changing, with calm waters one day and turbulent waves the next. As the captain, you must regularly check your compass to ensure you're on course. This compass is your gratitude practice.

Imagine you're Sarah, a small business owner who has made it her mission to express gratitude daily. Each evening, Sarah reflects on her day, noting down moments she's grateful for. But after a while, she notices her entries become repetitive, almost mechanical. It's a signal that her gratitude practice needs a reset.

So, Sarah decides to change her approach. Instead of just writing down moments, she starts to actively seek out new experiences to be thankful for. She takes different routes to work, strikes up conversations with strangers, and volunteers at local events. Each new experience brings a fresh perspective and a renewed sense of gratitude.

Sarah's reflection shows her that gratitude isn't a static practice; it's a dynamic process that requires attention and intention. By resetting her approach, she keeps her gratitude practice vibrant and meaningful. It's a reminder that, just like the captain must adjust the sails to the changing winds, we must adjust our gratitude practices to the evolving rhythm of our lives.

So, make it a habit to regularly assess your gratitude practice. Adjust as needed. Life's dynamic, and so is gratitude.

5. Gratitude in Adversity: Gratitude in adversity is like finding a beacon of light in the darkest of nights. It's the inner strength that allows you to see beyond the immediate storm and appreciate the journey, no matter how treacherous the path may seem.

Consider Alex, a startup founder whose dream project hit a major roadblock when investors pulled out at the last minute. With the future of his company hanging by a thread, Alex found himself at a crossroads. Instead of succumbing to despair, he chose to embrace gratitude. He gathered his team and expressed his heartfelt thanks for their hard work, their belief in the vision, and their willingness to take risks. He was grateful not for the setback, but for the opportunity to lead, to innovate, and to learn from the challenges.

This act of gratitude in the face of adversity became a turning point for Alex and his team. It fostered a culture of resilience, where every obstacle was viewed as a chance to grow and every failure as a lesson in disguise. The team rallied, found new solutions, and eventually secured the funding they needed.

By being thankful for the opportunity to play the game, Alex demonstrated that gratitude isn't just for the times of triumph; it's a powerful tool for navigating the trials of life. It's about appreciating the chance to pursue your passions, make a difference, and be part of something greater than yourself, even when the odds are stacked against you.

6. Never Settle: Gratitude isn't just a fleeting feeling; it's a deep-seated practice that shapes who you are and who you become. It's like being a sculptor, chiseling away at a block of marble day after day. You don't settle for the rough outline of a figure; you commit to the lifelong pursuit of refinement, detail, and beauty.

Take, for example, Maria, a seasoned photographer. When she started her career, she was grateful for any gig she could get. But as she honed her craft, her vision expanded. She didn't settle for the status quo; she pushed the boundaries of her art, capturing stories that went unnoticed. Each photo was a step in her journey, a testament to her evolving skill and her deepening appreciation for the world around her.

Maria's gratitude grew with every snapshot, not just for the successes but for the whole process—the early mornings, the missed shots, the learning curves. She understood that gratitude is the lens through which she sees the world, a lens that brings everything into focus, from the grand vistas to the intricate details.

Never settling means embracing gratitude as a core part of your identity. It's about recognizing that every step, every challenge, every triumph is part of a larger masterpiece you're creating with your life. And with each stroke of gratitude, you're not just checking off a box; you're rewiring the brain, therefore carving out a legacy.

There you have it! By embracing these practices, you're not merely adopting a habit; you're altering the very fibers of your being. This is the art of embedding gratitude into your biological makeup—making it a part of your subconscious, your reflexes, and your daily existence. It's the ultimate alchemy of the soul, turning every experience, challenge, and triumph into a precious metal of immeasurable worth. So, let gratitude be the heartbeat of your life, pulsing through every action, thought, and interaction.

## Overcoming Challenges to Gratitude

*"The greater the obstacle, the more glory in overcoming it."* - **Molière**

# Common Obstacles to Gratitude

Gratitude is the high-octane fuel that powers the engine of life, propelling us forward with joy and purpose. It's what keeps our spirits running at peak performance, driving us to overcome obstacles and reach new heights. But just like any finely tuned engine, there are factors that can introduce gunk into the system, impeding its efficiency and flow.

Think of gratitude as the clean, renewable energy source for your soul's engine. When it's abundant and pure, you feel unstoppable, capable of cruising through life's highways with ease and confidence. However, life isn't a straight, open road. It's full of stop signs, potholes, and unexpected detours that can challenge even the most grateful heart.

These challenges are like the carbon deposits in an engine. They can cloud your perspective, dampen your spirits, and create friction in your internal workings. Well, let's get right into it – common obstacles to gratitude and how they sneak up on you:

- **Entitlement:** This is a big one. Entitlement is like a sneaky shadow that follows you around, whispering sweet nothings about how you're meant for greatness just because you exist. It's a tricky mindset that clouds the clear waters of thankfulness and can creep up on anyone, convincing you that success should fall into your lap like ripe fruit from a tree, without the need to climb or even shake it.

But here's the raw deal – the world doesn't work on a 'just show up and get a trophy' basis. Success is not a door that opens with the mere tap of a finger; it's a fortress that requires a siege of relentless effort, strategy, and sometimes, the stars aligning in your favor. So, when you replace entitlement with gratitude, you shift from a mindset of 'deserving' to one of 'appreciating'—from expecting to be given to being thankful for what you have earned and learned along the way.

- **Comparison:** In today's digital age, social media is the grand stage where everyone presents their greatest hits. It's a constant stream of perfect vacations, flawless selfies, and personal triumphs. But what we don't see behind those snapshots is the reality—the outtakes, the bloopers, the effort behind the scenes. It's like comparing your behind-the-scenes footage with everyone else's highlight reel, and it's a game you can't win.

Gratitude gets lost in this sea of comparison. When you're scrolling through your feed, it's easy to feel like your grass is just not as green, forgetting that it might just be a filter. This is where you need to pause and remember that gratitude starts in your own backyard. It's about watering your own grass, appreciating the daisies among the dandelions, and realizing that every patch of lawn—yours included—has its own unique beauty and worth.

- **Busyness:** Busyness has become the modern-day currency of worth, where being perpetually 'on' is equated with being productive and successful. But this relentless pace is like a roaring waterfall, drowning out the gentle whispers of gratitude that remind us of life's true value. In the rush to do more, be more, and have more, we often miss the quiet moments of triumph and joy that truly enrich our lives.

Gratitude is a delicate melody that requires a pause in the orchestra of life to be truly appreciated. It's in these pauses that we can reflect on the small wins—the smile of a child, the completion of a project, the warmth of the sun on our faces. These everyday miracles are the notes that compose the soundtrack of a fulfilled life, but they're easily missed if we're constantly chasing the next big thing.

- **Negativity bias:** Negativity bias is like a glitch in the human software, a prehistoric code that once served us well when danger lurked behind every bush. It's the mental equivalent of a smoke detector that's a little too sensitive, going off at the slightest hint of trouble. This ancient alarm system can hijack our modern lives, making us hyper-aware of the negative and oblivious to the positive.

  But here's the kicker – we're not cavemen anymore. We're not on the menu for saber-toothed tigers. So, this constant scanning for threats? It's often just scanning for trouble where there is none. And that's where gratitude comes in—it's the update we need to install, the training program to debug the system.

- **Fear of Complacency:** The fear of complacency is like a ghost story told around the campfire of success; it's the chilling tale that if you dare to be grateful, you'll become content, and your ambition will wither like a vine without sunlight. But this is a myth, a misunderstanding of what gratitude truly is.

Gratitude isn't a cozy blanket that lulls you into a state of inaction; it's the spark that ignites a fire within. It's the recognition of the mountain you've climbed, not just to sit at the summit but to scan the horizon for new peaks to conquer. It's the fuel that powers the engine of progress, reminding you of how far you've come and how much potential lies ahead.

Imagine a climber; let's call her Zoe. She's reached the peak of a mountain after a grueling ascent. She stands at the top, breathless, taking in the view. She's grateful for the strength in her limbs, the resilience in her spirit, and the trail she's blazed. But Zoe doesn't pitch a tent to live on the summit. Instead, she uses that moment of gratitude to stoke her ambition, to look out at the range of mountains beyond, and to plan her next adventure.

Gratitude, in Zoe's world, is the compass that points her to her next challenge. It's the acknowledgment of her achievements that propels her forward, not into complacency, but into the thrill of the unknown and the promise of even greater accomplishments.

So, there you have it. The roadblocks to gratitude are real, but they're not insurmountable. It's about sharpening your awareness, shifting your attitude, and taking deliberate action. Recognize the barriers for what they are—mere distractions on the path to a more thankful existence.

Failing to dismantle these barriers can lead to a life and business that are stifled and unfulfilled. Without overcoming these obstacles, the potential for growth, joy, and success remains locked away. The energy that could be used to propel you forward is instead consumed by the weight of unaddressed challenges, leaving you stagnant. It's like running with a parachute; you might move, but not nearly as fast or as freely as you could. The power of gratitude goes untapped, and the extraordinary life that could be yours remains just out of reach.

## Strategies for Overcoming Negativity

Ever heard the quote by Elbert Hubbard – "*When life gives you lemons, make lemonade.*"? This famous quote serves as a timeless call to optimism and resilience. It's about taking the unexpected hardships—those sour, tart lemons—and transforming them into something positive and desirable, like refreshing lemonade. This metaphor is a powerful strategy for overcoming negativity because it encapsulates the essence of proactive positivity.

Making lemonade out of lemons means not just accepting the setbacks that come your way but actively seeking ways to turn them into advantages. It's about finding the hidden opportunities in every problem, the silver lining in every cloud. When faced with negativity, whether it's a personal setback, a professional obstacle, or just a general sense of pessimism, the "lemonade" approach encourages you to look for constructive solutions and to focus on the potential for positive outcomes. It's a mindset shift that turns obstacles into opportunities.

Imagine a seasoned athlete who suffers a career-threatening injury. Instead of wallowing in negativity, they use the recovery period to mentor young athletes, sharing their knowledge and experience. They start a podcast to discuss overcoming adversity, which gains a following and inspires others. Their injury becomes a platform for a new kind of leadership, transforming a personal setback into an opportunity to empower and uplift others. This exemplifies the essence of overcoming negativity. Now, let's explore some highly effective strategies.

- **Embrace the Suck:** "Embrace the Suck" is like a battle cry for the warriors of life. It's about standing tall in the face of adversity and taking it head-on. Life isn't a smooth ride;

it's a rollercoaster with ups, downs, and loop-de-loops. Those curveballs? They're not just random pitches life throws at you; they're tests of your mettle, your resilience, your ability to adapt and overcome.

When life hurls a fastball that knocks the wind out of you, you've got two choices: you can either step out of the batter's box, or you can stare down the pitcher and get ready for the next throw. Embracing the suck means you dig your cleats in, adjust your grip, and swing with all you've got. It's about transforming the energy of that pitch, the force of the impact, into your own power to hit it out of the park.

Take the story of a young entrepreneur, Mia. Her first startup went belly up, leaving her with debts and doubts. But instead of letting it defeat her, she embraced the failure. She dissected every mistake, learned every lesson she could, and came back with a new venture. This time, armed with experience and a no-quit attitude, she turned her past 'suck' into her present success.

That's the spirit of embracing the suck. It's not about enjoying the struggle; it's about valuing it. It's about knowing that every bruise is a badge of honor, every failure a stepping stone to success. So, when negativity comes knocking, you don't just open the door; you kick it down and say, "Thanks for the workout."

- **Audit Your Circle:** Take a hard look at who you're spending time with. This is a call to action, a prompt to evaluate the company you keep with the same scrutiny as a financial audit. It's about taking stock of relationships and measuring their value in terms of personal growth and happiness.

Imagine you're the captain of a ship, navigating the vast ocean of life. Your crew—the people you surround yourself with—can either be skilled sailors who help you steer through storms or mutineers who threaten to sink the ship. If your first mate is always pointing out the leaks and never helping to bail the water, it's time to promote someone who will grab a bucket and start scooping.

Think of Elon Musk in the early days of SpaceX. He surrounded himself with a team that not only shared his vision but also had the drive to achieve what many thought impossible—reusable rockets. This circle of positivity and ambition was crucial in overcoming the many failures they faced. Each setback was seen not as a defeat, but a step closer to success.

So, in essence, Auditing Your Circle is about ensuring that those around you are not anchors but sails, helping you move forward, not holding you back. It's about fostering relationships with those who share your zest for life and your thirst for achievement, who can laugh in the face of adversity and dream in the realm of possibility.

- **Content Diet:** Just like you watch what you eat, watch what you consume mentally. The idea of a "Content Diet" is all about curating what we feed our minds. It's the practice of being selective with the media we consume to ensure it positively impacts our thoughts, emotions, and behaviors.

    Imagine your mind as a garden. What you plant in it, you will eventually harvest. If you sow seeds of sensationalism, fear, and negativity—often found in certain news outlets, social media, or dark-themed podcasts—that's what will grow. Over time, these can crowd your mental space like weeds, overshadowing the more beneficial plants.

Now, think about planting seeds of knowledge, motivation, and positivity. Choose content that acts like sunlight and water, nurturing those seeds. This could be an enlightening documentary, an educational YouTube channel, or a podcast that explores human triumphs and innovations. Such content doesn't just passively sit in your mind; it germinates, grows, and bears fruit in the form of new ideas, a more positive outlook, and an enriched perspective on life.

For example, instead of tuning into a podcast that dwells on the problems of the world, you might listen to one that discusses solutions and breakthroughs. This doesn't ignore the reality of challenges but focuses on progress and potential, which can be incredibly uplifting and empowering.

In essence, a "Content Diet" is about making conscious choices to engage with media that contributes to your well-being and personal growth, much like a balanced diet contributes to your physical health. It's about ensuring that the content you consume serves you well and supports the life you want to lead.

- **Action Over Anxiety:** When you're feeling negative, get moving. "Action Over Anxiety" is a powerful mantra that encourages us to channel our restless energy into productive activities. It's about transforming the nervous, jittery feelings that come with anxiety into a driving force for positive action.

Let's say you're an aspiring writer who's feeling overwhelmed by the blank page in front of you. The anxiety of not being able to produce anything worthwhile is creeping in. Instead of succumbing to those feelings, you decide to take action. You set a timer for twenty minutes and start writing, no matter what comes out. Before you know it, the timer goes off, and you've got a few paragraphs on the page. The act of writing has shifted your focus from anxiety to creation.

This principle applies to any area of life. Feeling anxious about an upcoming presentation? Dive into researching and preparing your slides. Worried about a personal goal? Break it down into small, actionable steps and start tackling them one by one. By moving forward and staying active, you're not giving anxiety a foothold. You're too busy making progress and building momentum. That's the essence of

"Action Over Anxiety." It's about using action as a tool to overpower the negative thoughts and keep you moving towards your goals.

Negativity, much like an uninvited guest, will inevitably come knocking at your door. But you don't have to invite it in for dinner. Use these strategies, keep your head up, and stay grinding. That's how you overcome negativity and keep soaring to new heights. Now, go out there and show negativity it picked the wrong fight.

## Dealing with Gratitude Objectors

Gratitude is undoubtedly the real deal, but not everyone's ready to embrace it. You've got skeptics, naysayers, and the 'too cool for school' crowd who think gratitude is all fluff. But guess what? They're missing out.

These individuals often view expressions of gratitude as unnecessary, insincere, or even as a sign of weakness. They argue that success is born from hard work and individual merit, not from a mindset of thankfulness. They may see gratitude as a distraction from the 'real' factors that drive achievement, such as talent, intelligence, and effort. To them, saying "thank you" is superfluous — a social nicety rather than a meaningful gesture.

When faced with gratitude objectors, it's important to approach the situation with empathy and understanding. Here's an example:

Imagine you're the CEO of a startup, and you've implemented a culture of gratitude within your company. You encourage your team to express thanks to their colleagues, celebrate small wins, and reflect on positive experiences. However, Alex, one of your senior developers, doesn't buy into this culture. He believes that results should speak for themselves and that gratitude is just fluff.

Instead of dismissing Alex's perspective, you decide to have a one-on-one conversation with him. You listen to his concerns and acknowledge his point of view. Then, you share research-backed evidence on how gratitude can improve workplace morale, increase productivity, and even enhance overall well-being. You also provide examples of successful companies that thrive on a gratitude-rich culture.

To address his skepticism, you propose a 30-day gratitude challenge. Alex is asked to write down three things he's grateful for at the end of each workday. Reluctantly, he agrees to give it a try.

Over the course of the month, you notice a subtle shift in Alex's attitude. He starts participating in team celebrations and occasionally expresses appreciation for his colleagues' help. At the end of the challenge, Alex admits that while he still values hard work and results, he has come to see that expressing gratitude doesn't diminish those efforts. Instead, it creates a more supportive and enjoyable work environment.

Let's look at another scenario. Picture yourself grabbing coffee with your friend after a long workday. As usual, they launch into a tirade about their job – the endless hours, the demanding boss, the monotonous tasks. They're stuck on the complaint train, and it's full steam ahead.

Now, you've got two choices here: hop on board or lay down new tracks. Let's go with the latter.

You acknowledge their frustration because, let's face it, we've all been there. But then, you pivot. You share a slice of your day – not the deal you closed or the project you aced, but the moment you felt grateful for. Maybe it was the morning sun streaming through your office window, the team lunch that turned into a brainstorming session, or the mentor who took a moment to encourage you.

Your friend pauses, the complaints simmering down. They're listening, really listening, for the first time in what feels like forever. You're not dismissing their feelings; you're offering a different lens to view them through. It's not about being overly optimistic; it's about recognizing the good amidst the grind.

These examples illustrate how you deal with a gratitude objector. You don't argue or dismiss; you empathize and share. Now, let's elaborate on this approach to provide you with a comprehensive game plan:

- Acknowledge Their Perspective: When you encounter someone who's resistant to the concept of gratitude, it's often because they've had experiences that have shaped a more cynical view of the world. They might have faced disappointments or setbacks that make it hard for them to see the value in being grateful.

  Acknowledging their perspective is about recognizing that their feelings are valid, even if they differ from your own. It's not about trying to change their mind or convince them that they're wrong. It's about accepting that their experiences have led them to a different viewpoint.

  The key here is to coexist with these objectors without conflict. You're not there to challenge their skepticism head-on; you're there to offer a different perspective through your actions and words. By demonstrating how gratitude has positively impacted your life, you provide a living example that might, over time, influence their outlook.

In essence, it's about respect and understanding. You're not dismissing their skepticism; you're simply showing them another side of the coin.

- Keep It Real: Keeping it real with gratitude means embracing authenticity in your approach to life's challenges. It's about acknowledging the difficulties you face without letting them define you. Instead of glossing over the hard times, you find value in them by identifying the lessons learned or the strengths gained. Gratitude, in this sense is not a denial of problems but a recognition of the growth they foster.

By sharing your own struggles and how a grateful mindset has helped you overcome them, you offer a genuine narrative that others can relate to and be encouraged by. This honest reflection can be a powerful testament to the resilience that gratitude can build within us. It's a reminder that even in the midst of adversity, there are aspects of our lives and experiences for which we can be truly thankful.

So, sugarcoat nothing. Gratitude isn't about ignoring the tough stuff; it's about finding the silver lining. Share those struggles and how gratitude helped you navigate through them.

- Engage with Empathy: Engaging with empathy when facing resistance is about connecting on a human level. It's recognizing that everyone's journey is different and that adopting a new mindset, like one of gratitude, can be a significant shift. Empathy involves putting yourself in their shoes, understanding the emotional hurdles they might be facing. It's not about convincing them to change instantly; it's about being present, listening, and showing compassion.

When you approach someone with empathy, you're not dismissing their resistance; you're acknowledging it and offering support as they navigate through their own process of change. It's a gentle, patient, and understanding way of being there for someone, even when they're not ready to embrace the concept of gratitude fully. This approach can create a safe space for open dialogue and potentially pave the way for a gradual shift towards a more grateful perspective.

- Stay Consistent: Consistency in gratitude is like watering a garden. You can't just water it once and expect it to flourish; it needs regular care. Similarly, gratitude needs to be nurtured continuously to grow. Over time, as people around you observe the steady presence of gratitude in your actions and attitudes, they begin to notice the subtle yet profound impact it has. They see the resilience it builds, the relationships it strengthens, and the satisfaction it brings to everyday life.

  By maintaining a consistent practice of gratitude in the midst of its objectors, you're not just hoping they see its worth; you're showing them, day in and day out, through every thank you, every moment of reflection, and every acknowledgment of the good that exists even in the face of challenges. It's this unwavering commitment to gratitude that can inspire them to consider its place in their own lives.

There you have it, your game plan on dealing with Gratitude Objectors. Always remember, it's not about changing their mind on the spot. It's about planting seeds of gratitude and showing them there's another way to look at life and work. Keep it real, keep it consistent, and let gratitude do its thing.

# CONCLUSION

## The Grateful Journey Ahead

As we turn the final page of this exploration into gratitude, we stand at the threshold of a new beginning. This book has been a compass, guiding us through the rich history, the transformative science, and the practical application of gratitude in our lives and businesses.

We've journeyed together from the roots of thankfulness in ancient traditions to the cutting-edge research that underscores its power. We've woven gratitude into the fabric of our daily routines, discovered rituals that anchor us in appreciation, and witnessed the profound impact it has on our mental well-being and our relationships.

In the realm of business and leadership, gratitude has stepped forward as an indispensable partner. It's no longer a mere courtesy; it's the heartbeat of a thriving organizational culture. This silent force breathes life into companies, lifting them to new heights where success is measured not just in profit, but in the respect and admiration garnered from every corner of the enterprise.

Gratitude is the key that unlocks a culture of appreciation, a world where each individual is seen, heard, and valued. It's the foundation upon which customers are not just served, but genuinely cherished. In this realm, leaders who lead with thankfulness don't just command—they inspire, creating ripples of positivity that transcend the workplace and touch every aspect of business.

Yet, the path of gratitude is not without its hurdles. We've confronted the challenges, strategized against the negativity, and learned to navigate the presence of those who may not yet understand gratitude's potential. But armed with the insights and real-world examples shared within these pages, we are prepared to meet these obstacles with grace and perseverance.

As you step forward from this reading experience, carry with you the knowledge that gratitude is more than a concept—it's a way of being. It is the thread that can weave together the tapestry of a life rich with fulfillment and a business brimming with purpose.

Let this book be a living document, one that you return to as a source of inspiration and guidance.

Let the stories resonate, the strategies take root, and the practices flourish. And above all, let gratitude be the beacon that lights your way to a future where potential is not just reached, but exceeded.

In gratitude, we find the key to unlock not just our own potential, but the collective potential of humanity. So, go forth with a grateful heart, and let the journey continue.

# THE AUTHOR:

The German National Birgit Maria Kemphues is based for almost 20 years in the United Arab Emirates.

Her love for the tradition and the people in the Emirates reflects her great social commitment to people, animals, flora, and fauna in the country.

Due to her positive mindset and inexhaustible energy, she has been considered a great encourager among the locals.

She is an ambassador to the country.

Birgit Maria is involved in the economic and scientific dialogue between Europe and the GCC focus on United Arab Emirates. The book "Shine and inspire others", it is a tribute to the friendships that have enriched my life and broadened my horizons.

It is the power of understanding, empathy, and love to bridge gaps, to break barriers, to unite hearts.

www.instagram.com/Birgit_Maria_Kemphues

www.Kemphues.com

Books on: https://amzn.to/3Q0GWk3

https://amzn.to/3Q0GWk3

More on: https://amzn.to/3Q0GWk3

www.ingramcontent.com/pod-product-compliance
Lightning Source LLC
Chambersburg PA
CBHW050304230526
45471CB00005B/2020